HYENAS

HYENAS

Alice L. Hopf

Illustrated with photographs

A SKYLIGHT BOOK

DODD, MEAD & COMPANY
New York

ACKNOWLEDGMENTS
The author wishes to acknowledge the work of Hans Kruuk and Jane Goodall, whose classic research on the spotted hyena is reported in their books. She is also indebted to Mark and Delia Owens, whose work and writings on the brown hyena have brought new understanding about the animals.

Library of Congress Cataloging in Publication Data

Hopf, Alice Lightner, date
  Hyenas.

  (A Skylight book)
  Includes index.
  Summary: An introduction to the commonly misunderstood hyena, a somewhat dog-like relative of the civet and the mongoose which has undeservedly become one of the most hated creatures in Africa.
    1. Hyenas—Juvenile literature. [1. Hyenas]
I. Title.
QL737.C22H65   1983   599.74′427   83-7332
ISBN 0-396-01881-9

For Ted Lightner
Dear nephew and close family member

Contents

1

The Spotted Hyena

The hyena is a very misunderstood animal. People have always given it a bad name. It was thought to be a cowardly creature that followed the lion around, watching for it to make a kill. When the King of Beasts was done eating, the hyena, people believed, would then dine on what was left. Since the hyena feeds on dead animals, it was feared that it might even dig up graves and eat dead humans. Also the spotted hyena has a strange and frightening voice. Its call has been described as a crazy laugh or scary whoops and moans. Such things have made the hyena

A spotted hyena

one of the most hated creatures in Africa. But most of it is not true.

There are three species of hyenas. The common spotted hyena (*Crocuta crocuta*), which lives almost everywhere in Africa south of the Sahara Desert, is the largest and the most numerous. The animals are colored in shades of brown, from dark to yellow, and their tails are black and bushy. Black spots cover the body and legs. As the animal grows older, the spots fade so that a very old hyena may have spots only on its legs.

Spotted hyenas are among the few mammals—animals that give milk to nurse their babies—in which the females are bigger than the males. They are large, heavy animals, the females weighing over 120 pounds and the smaller males around 107 pounds. The two sexes look so much alike that it is almost impossible to tell them apart. The females are not only larger than the males, but they look like them sexually.

There is a story about a zoo director who asked an African wild animal collector to send him six hyenas— three males and three females. The hunter wrote back,

A small group of hyenas assembled at a carcass. The adult female on the extreme left is the mother of the black cub in the foreground, and the larger female on the right is the mother of the seven-month-old cub in the middle. Only when a female is nursing is it easy to identify the sexes in the field.

11

saying that he could not find any females but was sending three males. By the time the animals arrived at the zoo, one of the so-called males had produced two babies!

This strange arrangement of the sexes among spotted hyenas has been a puzzle for scientists ever since it was discovered. A recent report by zoologist Laurence Frank offers some explanations. He found that the female hyenas have unusually high levels of the male hormone in their blood. The dominant female has the highest level, almost as high as a male. This hormone makes for larger size, aggression, and dominance in an animal. Thus male hyenas are subservient to the larger females, and the scientist found he could tell the sexes apart because the males were so nervous when near the females.

Because of these peculiarities, early writers, from ancient times almost to the present, thought the hyena was hermaphroditic. That is an animal having both male and female sexes in one. The lowly earthworm can claim this distinction, but no known mammal. This myth about the hyena has been exploded. The females merely look like the males, but they are definitely female.

Because hyenas look so much like dogs and cats, some early observers thought they must be hybrids—a cross between the dogs (canines) and the cats (felines). Sir Walter Raleigh wrote in 1614 that the animals could not have been saved in Noah's Ark. God would only have saved the purebreds. He believed they were created after the Flood, by an unnatural mixture of dog and cat.

Today we know that hyenas are a distinct species, more closely related to mongooses and civets (family Viverridae) than to either dog or cat. Fossil bones of hyenas have been found in ancient rocks millions of years old, showing that the animals have evolved from a very ancient line. Hyenas have longer noses than cats, more like the dog. Their feet are also doglike, built for running and without the retractable claws of a cat. Their hindquarters slope down at the rear and appear weak. In spite of this, hyenas can run up to forty miles an hour when chasing their prey.

Hyenas have very strong jaws. They can even crack the huge bones of elephants, and they eat and digest most of the bones at a kill. Like dogs, they will eat almost any-

thing and this has given them the bad reputation of being eaters of garbage. However, in this they are useful to people. They clean up dead carcasses that might otherwise pollute the area. It is said that in some African villages, hyenas are encouraged to come in and keep the place clean. Holes are left in the walls or fences around the village so that hyenas can enter at night. But parents are careful to keep their children indoors after dark.

Pygmy mongooses in anthill den. The hyena is related to the mongoose.

2

Hunting

About twenty years ago, a young Dutch scientist Hans Kruuk began to study hyenas in the wild. To do this, he used a sturdy station wagon built to travel fast over rough country. With cameras, binoculars, and other scientific gear, he followed the hyenas around their territory. Since the animals hunt at night, his car was fitted out with all the necessities for eating and sleeping. He had to be ready to follow them at any time and under any condition.

He quickly learned that hyenas make their own kills. The myth of the cowardly hyena lurking behind the lion

Hyenas prey on zebras.

in search of a meal was exploded. He describes one hunt in which a group of hyenas killed an adult zebra. They had hardly started eating when two lionesses appeared and chased them away. Soon the lionesses were eating, while the hyenas stood around and watched. But not for long. One after another, the cheated hyenas rushed in and nipped the lionesses on their rears. In this way, they were able to chase the thieves away and get back to their meal. But then two big male lions arrived. All animals in Africa, with the possible exception of the elephant, give way to the male lion. The hyenas had to move to a safe distance and watch their meal being devoured.

As dawn was breaking, a busload of tourists drove up, all intent on photographing the lion at his kill. The scientist heard one lady remark about the hyenas, "Look at them—they're waiting for the spoils!" Only the scientist knew that it was the other way around. The lions had stolen from the hyenas.

Kruuk used another method of studying hyenas and

Spotted hyenas and vultures at a kill.

lions. He made recordings of the sounds of each when they were eating at a kill. When he later played the lion recording over a loudspeaker near some hyenas, the animals paid no attention to the sounds. But when he played the hyena recording, lions came running from a distance, looking for the hyena kill.

Since hyenas often prowl alone, they were once thought of as solitary beasts, living alone like the leopard or the tiger. But Kruuk's careful study changed that notion. He discovered that the spotted hyena is a social animal. Like humans, they live in groups. Each pack has its own territory which it defends vigorously. No other hyenas are allowed to hunt in the area or even to wander in, at the risk of being badly mauled. The animals mark the boundaries by leaving scent patches on rocks, trees, and bushes. Battles are often fought along the borders, each group trying to enlarge its territory.

3

Hyena Packs

All social animals have what is called a pecking order. Scientists first observed this in birds, but soon they realized that it is true of all animals that live in groups, including humans. The strongest animal rules the rest, and each one finds its place on down the line to the weakest. Sometimes the positions change, as one individual asserts itself to climb up to a higher position. But the system works to keep order in the group and prevent fighting. Hyenas have order and rank in their packs. Because females are larger than males, they stand at the top. One or two females are the leaders in each pack, with others ranged below. Males have rank and order, too, but the top male always defers

to the leading female. It is the female hyena that leads the pack on the hunt, that decides where and when to go. She takes her packmates on a boundary-marking expedition or rushes ahead into battle with the neighboring packs of hyenas. Frank found that dominant positions seem to be inherited. The offspring of the dominant female also ranks high in the pecking order.

Another scientist who has done a careful study of the spotted hyena is Jane Goodall. With her photographer-husband and their two-year-old son, they followed a group of hyenas over a two-year period. Dr. Kruuk used an anesthetic dart to capture hyenas he studied. He cut notches in their ears, thus helping him to tell individuals apart. But Jane Goodall found that each hyena has a different pattern of spots. There were about sixty animals in the group she studied and she soon learned to identify half of them. Others she could distinguish from the many photographs taken of each animal.

A group of spotted hyenas. Hyenas have order and rank in their packs, with weaker animals giving way to stronger ones.

One of her most exciting descriptions is of a battle between two neighboring hyena packs. It all started because
two hyenas were napping a bit outside the border of their
territory. Suddenly, eighteen members of the other pack
came running across the moonlit plain, led by the top female. One of the two intruders was quick and managed to
escape, but the rushing hyenas piled on top of the other
and began to tear him to bits. Screams, howls, and roars
pierced the night. But then ten of the neighboring hyenas
came hurrying to help the victim. They were within
their own territory and full of fight. They boiled over the
line and chased the attacking hyenas away. But as soon as
they passed the border and were on foreign soil, they be-
came uncertain and stopped. Then the owners of the area
rushed to attack and chased the others back across the line.
In this manner, the battle surged back and forth. The noise
they made—for hyenas are very noisy animals—attracted
more hyenas of each group. Before the battle ended, some
thirty or forty hyenas were fighting on each side. After

Each hyena has a distinctive pattern of spots.

twenty minutes, the animals gradually gave up and each group retreated into its own territory. But many had been wounded and at least one—the animal that started it all—would surely die from his many wounds.

4

~ِ◡رے

Communication

Animals like the hyena that live in groups must have some way of recognizing and communicating with each other. Hyenas have a complicated ritual for this purpose. They sniff each other's head and neck and lick each other, even inside the mouth. Or they may stand side by side, tail to front. Then each animal lifts its inside hind leg while the other sniffs under it. When a hyena lifts its leg for another to smell underneath, it is exposing its most sensitive area to the other animal's jaws. We see this gesture in fighting dogs and wolves. When the weaker gives up the battle, he lies on the ground, raises his leg, and exposes his neck to the victor. It is a sign of submission and rarely does the

27

Two young spotted hyenas. Hyenas have a complicated ritual for greeting, which includes sniffing one another.

victor take advantage. Hyenas have developed this behavior into an elaborate greeting ceremony.

When a wandering hyena returns to his pack, he goes first to the leading female if she is present. He sniffs at her and raises his leg for her to return the greeting. If the

Cubs are very active in greeting ceremonies. A seven-month-old spotted hyena cub is on the left, being approached by a six-week-old cub on the right. This is a very unusual photograph of a black hyena cub.

Ronald L. Tilson

leader is lying down she may yawn widely, as if bored with the whole thing. A lower-ranked animal pulls back its lips in a grin. Cubs are very active in greeting every adult that comes to visit.

Hyena life revolves around the dens. There are many holes in the African wild, dug by such animals as warthogs, jackals, and others. These are enlarged for dens by the hyenas. But as they are seldom large enough to accommodate an adult hyena, most of the digging is done by the cubs. Cubs are energetic and efficient diggers, and the dens, which are usually on flat ground, have numerous entrances and tunnels. Often there is a group of dens near each other. The dens extend far underground with many connections.

The cubs of several mothers play and grow together. Mothers often move the little cubs from den to den. They are playful babies and chase each other about and play tug-of-war with a stick or bone. The mothers lie outside, nursing the cubs when they are hungry and letting the

Two spotted hyena cubs at the entrance to their den.

little ones jump all over them with hardly a protest. Baby hyenas are well cared for by their mothers and are nursed for almost eighteen months. Hyenas do not bring food home to the den, as wolves and jackals do. Unlike those animals, they cannot eat at a kill and then go home and throw up the food for their babies. Occasionally, they may bring home a bone for the cubs to chew on, but that is all. And since a hyena kill is a violent and dangerous free-for-all, with each hyena trying to grab as much food as it can, the cubs are not taken on a hunt till they are well grown. Instead, they are nursed much longer than other wild babies.

By the time the hyena cub is six months old, it is often big enough to go on a hunt and eat along with the rest of the pack. But many cubs want to go on nursing long after that. They don't want to give up their mother's milk, even if there is another baby on the way. Often the cub is almost as big as the mother and when she pushes him away, he throws a tantrum. Jane Goodall describes one such instance. When the mother hyena refused to let her grown daughter nurse, the big animal began to squeal. It was a

Two adult females and a seven-month-old cub begin eating a male gemsbok that they have captured.

loud, harsh sound that went on and on. Then with her legs bent almost to the ground, she rushed round and round her mother, constantly screaming. She tried once more to nurse and received another nip. Then she ran off, still

Three nights later, very little is left of the carcass. The hyena on the left is an unsexed subadult and the one on the right is a young male associated with the group.

loudly howling. This battle of wills between mother and cub went on for weeks.

Hyenas do not have large litters. Usually there are only two. The mothers are very protective and keep close watch over their cubs. Male hyenas are chased away. A male might eat a young cub, especially if it belongs to a rival pack. For lone males often wander about in the wild. Even when the cub is old enough to follow the hunt and feed at the kill, the mother often stands by it and keeps other hyenas from taking its meat away.

5

~ِو

Young

Jane Goodall describes what happened to the top females of the group she was studying. One had recently given birth to twins and she and her friend, the next ranking female, were lying by the den one night when a group of seven hyenas from the neighboring pack raced up in an aggressive manner. It was two against seven, and the two females retreated while the invaders sniffed around the den where the babies were hiding. But mother love and territorial instinct soon took over and the two females turned and rushed back, their tails bristling aggressively. At this point, Jane drove her car a little closer to watch the action and the seven intruders ran off. She was never sure if it was the noise of the car that scared them or the females' steadfast defense of their den. The invaders knew they were off their home ground. But the next day the females moved the cubs to a den closer to the rest of the pack.

Hyena cubs are born well developed. They are little black bundles of fur. Their eyes are open and they already have most of their teeth. Soon they can even run a little. After feeding, they stumble about their mother and she cleans them off before sending them back to the den to sleep. Each day they become stronger and stay outside the den longer. By the time the mother has moved her cubs to the communal den, they are ready to play with the other young ones around them. Often the cubs of several mothers share the same den and they wander from one den to another in search of other cubs to play with.

Foraging male hyenas are not the only dangers faced by young cubs. Lions will make a meal of baby hyenas, given the chance. Jane Goodall once saw six lions approach the den that she was watching. Three mother hyenas were

lying close by, nursing their cubs. The top hyena first saw the lions and gave the alarm call. The five babies rushed down into the den and the three mothers ran off to a safe distance. The lions sniffed around the burrow before moving on. The big male lion stayed the longest, poking his nose down the hole and even making a few digging motions. When he finally left, the mothers rushed back, sniffing down the hole to be sure the cubs were safe. Then they ran back and forth for five minutes, sniffing and scent-marking all over. It was as though they wanted to cover the lion smell with a scent of their own. Finally, the babies came out again and life went on as before.

Jane cites another instance when a pair of courting lions settled down very near a group of hyena dens where thirteen young cubs were hiding. Lions do not eat when they are courting, but the pair stayed for more than two days. The hyena cubs could not come out of their dens and the mothers could not get in to nurse them.

Spotted hyena cubs of two different litters. Often cubs of different mothers share the same den.

© Leonard Lee Rue III

While lions are the greatest enemies of hyenas, the animals must also compete with other African predators. Chief of these are the great African wild dogs, which travel in packs about the plains. The dogs will not hesitate to take over a hyena kill if they can. And hyenas often try to sneak up on the wild dogs as they are feeding and grab a piece of meat. The outcome of such meetings is always uncertain. Kruuk once saw two hyenas usurp the kill belonging to nineteen wild dogs. Another time, he watched as five dogs chased five hyenas from a dead zebra they were eating. But soon two other hyenas arrived and chased the five wild dogs away. The wild dogs gave up and left and only then did the five original hyenas come back to feed. On still other occasions, he saw wild dogs and hyenas eating from the same kill, with only a bit of snapping and growling between them.

Leopards sometimes dispute a kill with hyenas, but it is usually the leopard's kill and the hyenas chase the leopard

The lion—the greatest enemy of the hyena.

up a tree. A much smaller predator is the jackal. Jackals are quick, clever animals that hang around a hyena kill and rush in to grab a piece of meat when they see the chance. Sometimes jackals eat side by side with the hyenas, ignoring the growls and snaps. If the hyenas stop eating long enough to chase them away, they come right back.

6

Socializing

Even adult hyenas seem to enjoy playing. Kruuk once watched four as they walked a short distance from their den to a deep pool in the river. There they splashed about, swimming and biting and pushing each other underwater with their front paws. Hyenas are not afraid of water and have been known to hide meat in a pond or water hole where it would be safe from other predators.

While female hyenas usually stay with the pack where they were born, the males often wander. Sometimes they even change from one pack to another. Jane Goodall tells the story of one young male, whom she named Quiz. This

hyena was about four years old and ranked high among the males of his age group. He even dominated some of the females of that group. One might think that he would be contented with life in his pack. But Jane watched him behave in a very unusual manner.

The hyenas of Quiz's pack had made a kill near the border of their territory. They made so much noise as they began to eat that thirty-nine hyenas of the neighboring pack came running. They gathered at the border, growling and whooping, and trying to get up the courage to cross into enemy territory and grab some of the food. But the uproar also attracted two lions that chased all the hyenas away and took over the kill for themselves. Now the two hyena packs sat on each side of the boundary and watched the lions eating. They walked back and forth with their tails curled up aggressively, but none of them dared to attack the lions.

Suddenly, Jane saw a lone hyena walk out into the area

Hyenas like water. Here one is cooling off in a pond.

between the two packs. It was Quiz, and he stood with his head up and his tail down, staring at the opposite hyena pack. Soon a youngster from that pack joined Quiz and the two went through the greeting ritual, rubbing each other's chin and sniffing under each other's legs. Quiz was in enemy territory and soon a group of eight hyenas moved toward him threateningly. He quickly ran back to his own group. There he went up to the leading female and greeted her, sniffing at her legs, licking her mouth, and bobbing his head in the way of a submissive hyena. He went on to greet in the same way the other adult hyenas of his pack.

Jane thought this would be the end of the incident. But, no. Twenty minutes later, Quiz repeated the whole thing, going through the greeting ceremony with several members of the neighboring pack until their leader chased him off. By the time the lions were done eating and had gone away, there were only five hyenas of the enemy pack still waiting. They rushed over to the carcass, but were chased off by Quiz's pack. The young male did not try to eat with his packmates, but crossed the line into enemy territory and lay down a short distance from the other hyenas.

On other occasions, he was seen eating and visiting with his neighbors. Once he even left a group of his relatives as they were marking the boundary of their territory. All alone, he ventured into enemy territory, stopping to watch and listen for a possible attack, but still going on, as though one pack did not satisfy his instinct for companionship.

7

The Striped Hyena

The other two species of hyenas are different from the spotted hyena in many ways. For this reason, scientists place them in a separate group or genus. They are the striped hyena (*Hyaena hyaena*) and the brown hyena (*Hyaena brunnea*). Both are smaller than the spotted hyena.

With these hyenas, the females are smaller than the males and are not the dominant sex. They have rather long, coarse fur and manes that go down the necks and backs

A striped hyena

and can rise up when the animals are excited. Their tails are longer and bushier than those of their spotted relatives. They have large scent glands under their tails and the sexes are easily recognized. The animals are not as powerfully built as the spotted hyenas and lack the strong, bone-crushing jaws. They do not hunt big game but eat small or medium-sized creatures and any dead animals they can find.

The striped hyena has a grayish coat with brown or black stripes. It lives in Arabia and India, as well as Africa and in western Asia, including parts of the Soviet Union. It is a nighttime animal. During the day, it rests in holes in the ground. It is never a threat to people, as the more aggressive spotted hyena can be. The animals live in much smaller groups than their bigger cousins. Often only two are seen together. They are easily frightened away from their food and will give ground even to vultures. If a dog attacks, they run. These are the animals that African villagers encourage to clean up their garbage. Besides feeding on refuse, the striped hyenas eat snakes and other reptiles, small mammals, birds, insects, and fruit.

8

The Brown Hyena

The brown hyena is an even rarer animal. It has been killed off in much of its original homeland. Now it is found only in southern Africa, where it is sometimes called the beach wolf. It has the habit of hunting along the beaches for dead fish and other sea creatures, including stranded whales. This hyena has a gray head, but its body is brown with a lighter mane down the back. The legs are striped, showing its relationship to the striped hyena.

Like all the hyenas, it relies strongly on its keen sense of smell. One observer in South Africa noted that when the animals are upwind of a food bait (with the wind blowing from them to the food), they will walk right past any food they cannot see. But as they move past it and get on the downwind side (with the wind blowing to them from the food), they will turn and go straight to the meat. One hyena scented a dried bit of meat from a mile away. Even little cubs have been observed to sniff often into the wind. But the hyenas were never seen to sniff downwind.

The brown hyena is even more solitary than the striped hyena and so shy that it only comes out after dark. During the day, it hides in rock crevices or warthog dens. A scientist who investigated its feeding habits found that it catches many small creatures such as locusts and hares. It also eats birds' eggs and some vegetation. The brown hyena does not have the crazy laugh of the spotted hyena. Instead, its call is a melancholy *wah-wah-wah*.

Mark and Delia Owens made a seven-year study of the brown hyena. They worked in the Kalahari Desert, a semidesert area in southern Africa. It is a harsh environment for all living things. During the dry season, from September to January, temperatures are often over 120° F, and the hyenas come out to hunt only at night. Food and water are so scarce that the hyenas do not live in packs, but each solitary animal searches for whatever prey it can find.

In their early days in the Kalahari, the Owenses lived in very primitive conditions. They slept in their Land Rover and nearby they had a drum of water and a campfire. To buy supplies, they had to drive to a town 150 miles away, and they saw other people only two or three times a year. In later years, as they attracted financial support for their work, they had several tents and even an airplane with which they were able to follow the animals they were studying.

In time the wild creatures grew used to the scientists and came right into their camp looking for food. The Owenses had to take special precautions to protect their food and stores. But even so they were often awakened by loud bangs during the night as the animals tipped over some object. Sometimes a hyena would come into camp in the dark and run away with a pot from the fireplace, carrying it in its mouth by the handle.

At night, Mark and Delia took turns getting up to shoo

Mark Owens

the hyenas out of camp. A gas lantern that made a hissing noise usually did the trick. But one night, when it was Mark's turn, he jumped out of bed without bothering to light the lantern. In his bare feet, he ran toward their camp and the animal that was making the noise. He could barely see it in the starlight. It was chewing up a framed screen that Mark had just made. Swinging his arms and shouting, "Go on . . . get out!" the man was barely four feet from the intruder when it rose to its feet—and Mark was staring at the biggest lion in the area!

The scientist froze, then slowly backed away, now muttering calming words. Being quiet, he managed to get safely back to his tent, while the lion carried the screen away into the desert.

Since brown hyenas are usually seen hunting alone, nobody realized that they are social animals, until the Owenses made their study. They were able to follow the animals at night and make note of where they went and

One-year-old brown hyena cubs greeting one another at their communal den in the Kalahari Desert of Botswana.

what they ate. The scientists learned that the hyenas of the area shared the same paths across the desert. They left scent markings for each other and came together to feed at abandoned lion kills. They had a pecking order, established by biting and shaking each other. Such behavior is not found among true solitary animals. The Owenses were able to immobilize some hyenas with anesthetic darts and then attach collars with radio transmitters. With this equipment, they were able to track the animals better and they soon found a communal den where several mothers kept their cubs.

One female hyena had a white patch on her forehead and the Owenses called her Star. They tracked her by radio and observed her activities as she raised her cubs and hunted in the semidesert for food. They were surprised to find that a brown hyena can chase a leopard from its kill or take over the kills of jackals and cheetahs. They also found that the animals eat small prey like lizards and rodents (rats and mice). But lions are their enemies, and Star was surprised one night and killed by the black-maned lions. The Owenses later found her remains.

They knew that Star had young cubs in an isolated den, and they went to watch where her three cubs waited. They would have liked to feed the hungry babies and help them in this emergency, but such actions would have spoiled their research. For a week they watched the den every night, as the babies waited for a mother that never came. The little ones sat forlornly at the mouth of the den, staring in the direction where their mother should come. Slowly, they grew thinner and weaker. Their hair fell out in patches for lack of their mother's milk.

Finally, the cubs stayed in the den and did not come out at all. The scientists crept up to the hole and listened, hoping that the babies were still alive. And that night their watch was rewarded. At midnight, they heard a faint sound outside the den. They saw another hyena, the cubs' half brother, come to the hole.

He was carrying a dead springhare, a kangaroolike rodent. He put it down at the entrance to the den. Then he called softly. The three little cubs, weak and hungry, staggered out of the den and welcomed him with excited cries. Even before they began to eat, they greeted their brother with delighted squeals. Then they dragged the carcass into the den to eat.

Every night after that, some adult hyena brought food to the three orphans. The Owenses had established beyond a doubt that the brown hyena is a social animal and will care for any neglected offspring of the clan. In this they differ from the spotted hyenas, which never bring food home to their cubs.

9

The Aardwolf

In Africa there is a relative of the hyena called the aard
wolf (*Proteles cristatus*). In many ways it looks like the
striped hyena. It has long legs and its back slopes down
toward the rear. It has a long mane and a woolly tail. Its
hair is grayish yellow, striped with black. But its teeth are
not like those of the hyena. They are small and widely
spaced and are more like those of an insect-eating animal.
The ancient Egyptians knew the aardwolf. Drawings of
the animal have been found in graves and on the walls of
tombs that are thousands of years old.

Insects are the aardwolf's main diet, especially termites. It has a very long tongue with which it licks up the insects. In Africa, termites build large mounds out of earth which become hard as cement in the sun. The aardwolf's weak claws cannot tear these mounds apart unless they have been softened by rain. In the dry season, the aardwolf has to wait until the termites leave their hills. Then it hurries to lick them up. When there are not enough termites, the aardwolf eats mice and moles and such creatures. The aardwolf's long tongue is quick and skillful. It is also used for grooming and is so long that it can reach up to the animal's eyes or under the lower jaw to clean those places.

Since termites are a pest to humans, great efforts are made to kill them. This is hard on the aardwolves, for their chief food is being destroyed. Also dogs take their toll. Native Africans have trained their dogs to hunt jackals, which they believe kill their sheep. But the dogs kill the aardwolves as well, making a rare animal still rarer.

Aardwolves are thinly spread over certain parts of Africa, always where their termite food is found. They do not live in forests or mountains. They are shy, night-dwelling creatures, usually alone, although sometimes as many as six may form a pack. They cannot run very fast, but they have a good defense in a gland that gives out a very bad smell. Like that of our skunk, this has proved to be a good protection.

Index